Marketing Maniac

//

How to Scale Your Online Business Fast

Table of Contents

Introduction 1

Chapter 1 - Million Dollar Mindset 3

    Right Mindset Re-Defined? 4

    What is the Law of Attraction? 6

    The first step to manifesting more 9

    Be very vigilant when your inner voice says you can't do it 11

    The Law of Attraction Centre of Your Brain: Reticular Activating System. 12

    This is how it works: 13

    RAS and the business 14

    Cybernetics 14

    What Can I Do? 15

    Visualization 15

    Create a Vision Board 19

Chapter 2 - Divide to Multiply 22

    Speed up the pace 25

    If you're not swift, your rivals will be swift 25

    Be the master of your mornings 27

    Stay out of technology for the first 30 minutes. 28

    Drop to the stillness 29

    What if I'm a night owl? 31

Create your own "workday." 32

Chapter 3 - Revise your Mission statement frequently 34

Is your mission statement still valid? 35

So, what is the Mission Statement? 36

Questions that you should ask when creating a mission statement. 36

When am I supposed to review my mission statement? 42

When a company makes changes to its mission statement, this usually indicates growth. 42

Chapter 4 - Social Media Marketing 46

What do you need to do before you start a social media marketing campaign? 46

Who is addressing the problems that your product solves? 49

Chapter 5 - Work on your business (not in it) 54

How to start automating your business 55

Create a budget 57

Create training videos 58

Share the vision 59

The hiring processes 60

Interview Sheet 61

Other places to look 62

Chapter 6 – Invest and reinvest (where to put your money within your business) 65

You need to prepare first. 66

Is it time to invest? 67

The Warren Buffet ideology 68

    Reinvestment...68

    How to Reinvest Your Profit...69

    Marketing and advertising..69

    Investing in outsourcing...70

    Invest in Yourself..71

Chapter 7 - Fall in love with failure 72

    Analyze and Change...73

    Leverage flaws and accept responsibility 74

    Analysis Paralysis...75

    Three simple steps for easier decision making:.........................75

    Check yourself 77

Chapter 8 - Expand Your Brand: In What Other Ways 79

    What's brand awareness?..79

    Brand awareness promotes trust...80

    Brand awareness creates an association....................................81

    Brand awareness builds brand equity...81

    How to Establish Brand Awareness 83

    Be a person, not an organization..83

    Socialize..84

    Tell a story..84

    Make it easy to share..85

    Brand awareness is about impact...86

    How To Boost Brand Awareness?..86

    Offer freemium. 86

    Make free content...87

Sponsor events.. 88
Give your brand a personality. 89
Produce podcasts. 90
Measure Brand Awareness 92
Quantitative Brand Awareness Measures 92
Qualitative Brand Awareness Measures.. 93

Introduction

Scaling up an online business is not rocket science-it's much easier than many people think. The sky's the limit when you combine a winning product or service with a solid foundation on which to build. To most individuals who have an online business, we all hope somewhere deep down that one day, and it will be self-sufficient, flourishing, and producing more than enough revenue to live off comfortably in itself.

Now, if you're a solopreneur, juggling your 9-5, social relationships, and self-care, scaling up your online business may sound like a "someday" kind of thing.

Fortunately for you, though, you can scale up your business without having to immerse yourself in hours of extra work every day because who's got the time? You can scale your business and earn more while saving time by taking advantage of these foolproof strategies I will share with you in this book.

What you'll discover in this book.

- What it means to scale your online business.
- How the million-dollar mindset works
- Smart investment: when and where to invest in your business
- Building a sure-fire brand for global visibility.
- How regular mission statement review helps to keep focus and value in the business.
- The thorough mental preparedness every business owner must have.

Fellow onlineprenuer, do you accomplish that much in your business as you think you should? Though starting an online business can seem almost instantaneous, it takes time for your varying inputs to yield amazing results. In this book, you'll learn some practical business lifestyle that will serve as a springboard for your business career and how you can give your business the needed lift and visibility. Let's dive in!

Chapter 1 - Million Dollar Mindset

Have you ever wondered why certain people can hop from success to success, without faltering? Nobody has the capacity, to be honest, but it may seem like that. Not surprisingly, to be successful, we need more than just motivational quotes. As an entrepreneur, there are certain qualities that are needed for success.

Fortunately, through dedication and a desire to develop, most of them can be trained, improved, and developed. Having this skill as an entrepreneur will allow you to deal with your day-to-day business more efficiently. And you're going to think-and act-like a real entrepreneur. We're going to address a very significant prerequisite for success in online business. It is, in reality, the significant and basic component of any productive venture. It is becoming more important for running an online business because of the complexity of the business involved. It is the most talked about and debated topic, but it is not well understood and often ignored. It's termed the MINDSET. If you have the right mindset, each task you do will bring the desired result—the mindset to flourish and accomplish.

Before you can get started with any new venture in life, you must first have the right mindset. If you are to quit smoking, you can't just buy a book on how to quit and expect it to be easy. You've got to be open-minded and eager to do what it takes, whilst also staying focused and never giving up. As easy as it may sound, we all know that it isn't at all. In fact, it takes an immense amount of determination in an all-around battle against yourself.

Much like quitting an old habit, forming new ones also takes a change of mindset and a new attitude. I am a firm believer in the Law of Attraction and manifestation, as I have used it for my own personal growth. I would like to introduce to you what this really means, in a very practical and science-based way so that you too can use it.

Right Mindset Re-Defined?

This is the continuous state of mind, charged with vibrant energy, which entrusts success or failure. Every major achievement is first accomplished in mind. You can't do what your imagination can't think of. Before you draw the conclusion, let me create a divide between the occasional wishful thinking and the mindset.

An idea is a drive that, if nurtured and developed, will channel events in order to begin the cycle of achievement. An idea could erupt from an occasional thought. Yet, this will be the end of it. You may develop an empire on your idea, but you need to fulfill what the idea perceives.

Your Mind is the center of that energy that is going to channel events. You've got an idea, and you're firm that it's going to work. If you have the right mind, you're going to believe that you can make it work. It is the self-confidence that distinguishes the mind as a wholly different entity from the occasional thinking.

It's because you can only achieve what you've achieved in your mind. It sounds like a paradox, but it's not. No matter who you are or what you do, you can't go beyond the threshold that you put on your mind. There're so many people on this planet who fantasize about becoming rich, but never will. Now, this is traceable to their mindset.

Let's say you want to make a million dollars. How will you go about that? First and foremost, it starts with the belief that you will actually make a million dollars. The main challenge is how you're going to go about it. There is a myriad of possible means. But first of all, you need to be persuaded that you're really going to make that million. If you're absolutely positive, then you can truly feel like you've got millions. No, I'm not writing here about any sort of megalomania. But the condition where you can picture yourself to be like a millionaire. It's a condition where you can almost sense the accomplishment of you, given whatever your financial status is. You are no longer skeptical of your success. Sure! It's going to take time, but you've already grown out of your allowed limits, and that is the primary requirement.

As you transition into the business that will bring the harvest, your mindset is further bolstered. The more relaxed you are, the clearer your vision and actions will be. Everything flows perfectly when you've got the right mindset.

What is the Law of Attraction?

The "Law of Attraction" is a phrase coined by the author of the book "The Secret". It tells us that a positive mental attitude brings us positive experiences, while a negative mindset brings us negative experiences. An example used in "The Secret" is someone who is always thinking about debt will attract more debt. Even if you are constantly thinking about getting OUT of debt, because you are thinking about debt, you will attract it. The same is true if you are thinking about money. If your inner dialogue about money is always positive, then you will attract more money into your life.

Whether you're conscious of it or not, you're always talking to yourself. You have a thought, and you react either positively or negatively to that thought. Many of us prefer to "choose" a negative reaction because we personally respond to our thoughts. Breaking away to view the perception takes effort, critically, for most of us. Let's assume, for example, that you're about to start a new online business and that you're beginning to feel nervous. You already have an idea that you think might help to solve a specific problem that is scheduled for review at a meeting, but abruptly, your mind is overwhelmed with thoughts of self-doubt.

How are you going to respond? Would you take a pessimistic response to your thoughts (Response A) or be rational and choose a more constructive response (Response B)?:

Response A: I'd better keep my mouth shut. My idea probably isn't as good as I thought it was, and I'm just going to end up looking stupid.

Response B: I'm going to go ahead and present my idea. However, if it is dismissed, it demonstrates that I think constructively about the problem and seeks to contribute to the solution.

Response A secures failure because it means that you're not even going to risk trying. You responded, and you chose a negative, self-talk response. Response B, a positive choice, means you're willing to risk failure, and trust that either way, you're going to be alright. Positive self-talk is optimistic and assertive. The fact that you have this potential for inner discourse and the ability to guide it is essentially why the words you tell yourself count.

Telling yourself negative reports almost always leads to negative outcomes, and while optimistic perspectives on your thoughts don't always ensure success, they certainly point you in the right direction. Here's a bit of a lesson that successful people have learned: even more essential than what you say is how you say it. When you can learn how to step back and analyze interaction from a third-person viewpoint, you'll have a much easier time to react positively to negative thoughts. For instance, Brené Brown, a motivational speaker, who also doubles as a professor at the University of Houston Graduate College, refers to the negative "thoughts" in her head as her "gremlins." In so doing, not only does she dissociate herself to gain some insight, she even makes fun of them! Starting to learn how to be rational about the ever-present thoughts in your head may take some practice at first, but when it becomes a habit, it will become intuitive, and you will find your life - both personal and business - changing in significant ways.

The first step to manifesting more

Are you conscious of the force of your inner dialogue? If you're not, just stop reading and listen for a moment. It's the inner voice that's always talking to you. The chances are that you have overlooked this little voice, and if you have, it means you've skipped a very significant element in manifesting your desires. Your inner dialogue is a very effective tool for creating your own self-belief.

Your inner voice can be either good or evil. If you are typically a positive thinker, a cheerful person, then your inner voice is more than likely to be optimistic. You're going to have the pleasure of healthy living. Unfortunately, most people do not have a positive thought habit; their inner voice is pessimistic. While these people may be trying very hard to improve their situation, they are simply pulling back from their own pessimistic inner dialogue. And they're always wondering why nothing really changes in their lives.

How much success and personal satisfaction you have achieved in your life is directly proportional to your inner dialogue. When you're always having a pessimistic conversation within your head, you'll find that sadly no amount of affirmations can bring any noticeable changes in your life. Since your inner discourse is so important to your self-development, you will have to have an insight into the role it plays. Your inner voice is actively judging and evaluating. All you see, hear, or feel in your inner chatter gives you an opinion, right or wrong, good or bad. This evaluation is, of course, based on your previous experience. It is really important for your life, of course. When you see a snake, for example, your inner voice will warn you to be careful because there is a risk. When you see a flower, that inner voice will tell you that this is a very beautiful thing. As you've seen, your inner dialogue is very important; it plays the role of a guard, safeguarding you from danger.

However, inner dialogue is often not helpful in helping you grow your inner power. Maybe you have a habit of saying 'can't do that? If you do, I recommend that you completely delete this word from your vocabulary right now. Ok, this may be the best recommendation I've ever offered to you.

Be very vigilant when your inner voice says you can't do it.

In order to protect you from danger, your inner dialogue tends to avoid anything new. This has good intentions, it's helping to defend you, but at the same time, they have an unbelievably militating effect on your personal development. In order for you to develop, you will face new challenges. Suppose you intend to make a million dollars. You've never done this before, you've scanned the archive of previous encounters, but you can't find any matches. Your inner voice will posit 'You Can't.' Not only that, but it's going to be very difficult to persuade you that it's unlikely for you to make the million dollars. You see, actually, it's trying to protect you. That may sound odd, but that's how your inner dialogue operates.

But to make that million dollars, you're going to be learning new skills, new ways of interacting with the world. Don't take the answer to your inner discourse for granted. Check it, because you cannot find the answers in your past experience archive. Is it true what it says?

Be aware of your inner dialogue and replace negative thoughts with positive thoughts. That's really everything you need to do to make your life good and fulfilled.

So, you're wondering, if it's that easy, why isn't everybody doing it? There's just one explanation, and it's because not everyone knows what's good and what's not good. When people face difficulties, they go out and buy books, search for mentors, go to workshops, gurus in hopes of solving their problems. Unfortunately, none of these things can change their issues if they do not change their approach.

Only if you know that the problem lies within yourself will you solve the problems of your life. When you don't remember anything else about what I've said, consider this: "There's a solution inside you to any one of your problems." You don't need to go outside to find solutions; the solution is already within you.

The Law of Attraction Centre of Your Brain: Reticular Activating System.

Your Reticular Activating System, or RAS, is the part of the brain that enables you to set and accomplish what you want in life. RAS works 24 hours a day, seven days a week, processing out all the information your brain receives.

Its sole purpose is to find what you want. So, you better KNOW what you want. You see, your brain has come to know you remarkably well over the years, and if some information is important to you, your RAS will make you aware of it. If you are a happy person, always searching for new opportunities, your RAS will help you find positive opportunities. Likewise, did you notice how pessimistic people always find the negative side of everything?

If you're excited to do something great, your RAS will prepare you in the best way possible — and help you to succeed. Similarly, if you're concerned about anything going wrong, your RAS will find ways to increase your worry and enable you to make it go wrong.

Your RAS is a "genie in a bottle." Your every desire (consciously or subconsciously) is his command. It does not know the difference between right and wrong. It just knows how to find out more about what you're focusing on. This is the idea behind the powerful Law of Attraction.

This is how it works:

If you're worried that you don't have enough money, that you're overweight, that you're always in the wrong relationship, or that you don't get enough output in your business, then your focus is on those factors. Your RAS will find a way to produce more.

Let's say you've just bought a new car, assuming it's the only one in town. Once you drive it around, you immediately begin to see the same model everywhere you turn.

RAS and the business

In business, RAS works the same way. That's why setting the RIGHT Business Goals is so critical. Set the right expectations and your RAS will begin to find ways to help you reach them.

Cybernetics

The goal here is to make sure you're concentrating on what's important to you. Still think about what you want to do. Your brain has a control and response system called cybernetics, which means "how the system works" which is found in some machines and animals.

Here's an example of how it works: do you know that, as a general rule, the airplane is 99 percent of course? Each time it deviates from its path, its cybernetic system sends a signal to the automatic response system to get it back on its programmed route.

The brain's got the same system. Due to this system, the strangest things are executed by those who are not trained for success. They'll win lotteries, then end up wasting all the money. They're losing weight, and they're getting it all back. In business, that's why people work incredibly long hours, or accept second best, even though they know they can do a lot better! You've already been programmed, based on all your past conditioning and old paradigms.

What Can I Do?

Try to take a look at your current business situation. Might well need to change? However, if you do not rewire your business programming, you will revert back. So, begin by taking the next 5 minutes to analyze your RAS and your own cybernetic mechanism — and adjust it to what you desire! Then work on it by maintaining your focus on what you want to do more. Your RAS is going to do the rest.

Visualization

'What the mind can conceive and believe, it can achieve'

-Napoleon Hill

The very profound thought that Napoleon Hill presents above represents the nature of one of the essential strategies in self-help for entrepreneurs. It is considered a creative visualization. Creative visualization encourages business leaders to conjure up, in their minds, images of the state of commercial affairs that they would want to be in reality. As most, if not all, the world's businessmen go to bed at night, they still find themselves wide awake even long after their family is probably asleep. They are concerned about how to scale their business, how to clinch that multi-million-dollar contract, or even what new product niche to pursue.

But these moments offer useful opportunities for business executives to indulge in innovative imagination to help their minds think of new strategies to maximize their business's sales and consequently their income.

The concept of "creative visualization" is made up of two main words: 'creative' and 'visualization.' Creative is an adjective conjugated (formed) from the infinitive 'to create' that means to make up or build. In addition to building in this sense, however, one does so according to one's own standards or requirements. In other words, it is normally motivated by an individual's own goals or motives.

The second part of the statement is visualization, which means seeing (to see). When you visualize something that you see in your mind, you create the image(s) of it. In such a scenario, it still does not exist. In fact, as it is just in your mind. Nevertheless, the main purpose of this technique as a self-help concept for business gurus is that it motivates them to create mental representations or blueprints (in their minds) of situations that they want to come about or happen one day (or at a set period). Hence, creative visualization is like a mental map or strategy that has not yet been conveyed from the mind to another state.

Imagine that you're going to build a house. Suppose you are not an expert in this type of profession. This means that you're going to have to engage a professional builder and tell him/her what you want. How are you going to let the builder know precisely what you want? First, you have to visualize the completed house imaginatively. The doors, the windows, the kitchen, the balcony, the bedrooms, the roof, the type of the structure, the texture of the walls, the finishing paint, and other components.

Try out your ideas by visualizing them in action.'- David Seabury. As Seabury suggests, after conjuring up the shapes and form in your mind and seeing the completed structure, you can then start to put it on paper, whether you sketch it roughly yourself, or get a structural engineer to do it professionally for you.

Entrepreneurs and business leaders should take a similar approach when thinking about setting smart objectives for their businesses and developing strategies to achieve them. Once they follow this path, this will afford them the opportunity to explore a lot of ideas in their own minds before trying to integrate them into their strategic business plans. During the visualization process, they will have a chance to see these ideas in practice and develop the acumen to determine whether or not they are likely to be appropriate for their enterprise.

Don't forget that, ... You've got to see it first before you can do it.

In the meantime, creative visualization makes use of an entrepreneur's windows to the world; that is, it utilizes all the sensory receptors. And, to visualize a situation, one has to use the senses of smell, seeing, hearing, tasting, and touching to do so.

A business owner will not obviously have to use all the senses in every situation, but it is pertinent that he/she knows that they are the faculties that one uses to evoke mental images.

And when one visualizes (e.g. building a house), one is persuaded to do so as if one is living in the reality of what that individual is visualizing. Feel the sensations that are going with the real situation, hear the sounds that are going to be related to the real situation (knocking and drilling of the walls), smell any natural scents that will be there (cement), feel the texture of the wall, etc. I use the building of a house as an illustration because I feel it would be a scenario that most of you would be able to relate to. Even if you've never built a house before, you shouldn't find it hard to picture such a scenario.

You must first practice visualizing simple situations and, as you become comfortable with the technique, motivate yourself to more advanced exercises. The last thing you want to do is devote precious business resources (money, personnel, equipment, and time) to projects and strategies that are practically unachievable. And hence, you need to ensure that henceforth this will become a new technique that you can use to maximize your chances of getting something you really want out of your business. Remember, whatever your mind can conceive and believe it can accomplish.

Create a Vision Board

I'm a firm believer in vision boards. I believe that what you see as well as what you believe can become a reality. A vision board is a collage of photos that portray what you want in your life. Most people use poster boards to make their vision boards. The number of items you want on your board will determine the size of the poster board that you need. One of my favorite vision board practices for those engaged in network marketing is to take their business's magazine and cut out the pages of those individuals the business recognizes, then add your picture to that list.

If you are making a list of high-achievement names, add your name to the list. Such stuff needs to be close to your office. Your vision board will be on the wall behind your office, so you're constantly reminded of where you want your picture and your name. Is there a ride that you'd like to take? You might want to visit a state or a country you've never been to before. Get some pictures and maps of the area and place them on your vision board. You might want to visit a family that you haven't seen for a while. Get the images of them and submit the pictures to your dream board.

Do you like your car? Is there another car you'd rather drive? Get a photo of the car on your vision board. Better yet, check the nearby dealer and get a photo of you right beside the car. Tell the dealer you are working on a business and you are working toward buying the car, and you'd like the photo. I know some people who have tried this; they've never been turned down for the photo.

What about your home? What would you like to change? Get some pictures of what you want on your vision board. Do you have your favorite quotes? I know a girl whose dream board is packed with meaningful quotes. These quotes help her to become the person she wants to be.

MARKETING MANIAC

Chapter 2 - Divide to Multiply

I wanted to share with you some very important information regarding time management and productivity. Wanting to scale your online business rapidly will not come easy, as you probably already know. But one of the most important keys to unlocking your potential as an entrepreneur is being able to control your own time.

The highest-earning people, the top-performing athletes, and the elite all have one very important thing in common. They have above-average time management skills, and they know how to optimize their productivity. Think about a production line in a factory. If the employer only has their worker for 8 hours on the line, then the only way to make more parts is for the employee to work faster.

Time management is one of the most crucial and yet one of the most challenging aspects of running a business. Time is still the only thing you can't replace, you can't purchase, and you can't recreate.

Whatever it is that you do online, the clock is always ticking, so you're always moving closer to your next deadline. For others, however, time is rarely a concern, and some appear to struggle to reach the simplest time limits. But by addressing your time constraints in a calculated and rational way, you can meet deadlines far more efficiently as and when they arise to create a better perception of you and your business.

Operating a business, online or offline, takes a certain level of admin and back-end time. No-one can actually work twenty-four hours a day, seven days a week on a lucrative, fee-earning work. Apart from the need to sleep, eat and relax, there's always a need to contact clients, stay on top of your accounts, figure out the next promotional campaign- all of which takes a lot of time. Consequently, the first rule in successful time management is to know exactly how much time you have on your hands at full capacity, before you start thinking about how accurately that time is to be allocated.

Arising from this is an important principle that you should never attempt too much work, or simply give unrealistic deadlines in order to satisfy clients. Know your time limits and how much you can manage physically. After all, there are only so many hours in the day, and some timelines will be physically impossible to meet.

Discipline is another approach to time management. Keep track of what you need to do, when you need to do it, and how long you need to do it. Then just stick to it. There is no reason to set deadlines for project completion if you do not plan to adhere to them-discipline yourself to work for a given period of time on a project and make doubly sure, whatever happens, that you deliver everything within your time limits. By being more disciplined and inspired, you will quickly notice that you've become more efficient, which can have a positive effect on earnings. Keeping time is a key aspect of professionalism and one that should be at the top of your priorities when running an online business. Although it can be tempting to get distracted or carried away with other things, keeping up with your pre-scheduled timings is the best way to manage your time efficiently, keep customers satisfied, and deliver on your business commitments.

Now, there are only 24 hours in a day, so you have to manage your time very effectively and learn how to regulate your energy to be productive. Note, time is time, and money is money, and nothing is more valuable than time. John Maxwell said, "Your success is determined by your daily agenda." Start planning your time today and start earning the money you really crave.

Speed up the pace

The most successful individuals in the world are in more of a rush to get to their goals than the average person. They wake up earlier, they think at a faster pace, and they don't waste time.

Ed Mylett is one of the top 50 wealthiest people under 50 and is the fastest-growing business personality in social media's history. In one of his videos, he talks about the depth perception and time management skills of max-out performers. I'd like to elaborate a little more on that.

We all know that entrepreneurs need to act swiftly to survive. It's in their blood; it's a natural impulse to move quickly. Still, the impact of speed in business is easy to underestimate. With the pace at which society is moving forward, businesses need to do whatever it takes to remain relevant.

If you're not swift, your rivals will be swift.

With the pace at which business moves, keeping up is a relentless task that will never be easier. Everyone out there is working faster than ever to take the next step swiftly, leaving you with little time to prove yourself. If you can't compete and move quickly, your rivals will. They're not going to think twice to leave you in the dust if you can't seem to think on your feet. As Jeff Lerner, founder and Executive director of Xurli, says, "In a world where everyone is moving so fast, merely being fast isn't enough; you must also be quicker than anyone and everyone else. Accelerate until you're at the front and act swiftly to stay there." Think of Blockbuster - they've remained the same for years, while their competitor, namely Netflix, has found ways to move the entire industry forward quickly. Obviously, it wasn't that good for Blockbuster. Carl Kustell, Buffalo's divorce lawyer, clearly pointed out, "The moment the word comes out that you're going to launch, expect someone to try to split the market. And if it works when you start, it's going to be copied. It's best to be quick.

People who understand exactly how close they are to their goals can move a lot more quickly and accurately to get there than the average person. A marathon runner will pace themselves at the beginning of the race because they know that the finish line is still far away. Once they get close to the end of the race, they can see exactly where the finish line is so they will begin to sprint. The closer you think you are to your goal, the faster you will run to get there.

The people that are winning in business have accurate depth

perception. They know exactly how close their goal is to them, and they are constantly sprinting to get there. These people are in a bigger hurry to get to where they're going. Evaluate your pace. How big of a hurry are you in? If you find yourself working at a slower pace, then re-evaluate your goals, and divide them up into smaller goals that are more easily attainable. Once you can see exactly where you are going, you can sprint towards that finish line

Be the master of your mornings

The way that you begin your day will dictate how you spend the rest of it. If you hit the snooze button over and over until you have to jump out of bed, get dressed in a panic and run out the door with a cold butter-less bagel, then you have already lost. This sets a very negative tone for the rest of your day psychologically. You want to make sure that you are starting the day on your own terms. This means putting your phone away and engaging in a quick morning ritual.

Your morning ritual can be anywhere from 30 minutes to an hour, depending on when you wake up. Your morning ritual should include food, exercise, and some form of goal setting and meditation. All of this should be done before you look at your phone to answer texts and emails. This will eliminate unnecessary distractions and allow you to take control.

The more change agents I meet and interact with, the more I see a set of constants in their lives. First is gratitude, the other is their ability to focus, and the significant one is how they organize their mornings. I realize there's a huge difference for me in the level of my effectiveness and productivity between the days I get out of bed, and the days I wake up with my mind already full.

When we prepare and schedule our morning hours, particularly the very first hour of the day, we set ourselves up for success. Of course, our path will be crossed by unanticipated and inconvenient challenges. How we start the morning is more than likely to decide how we meet, handle, and pass through these activities.

Stay out of technology for the first 30 minutes.

Don't freak out about it. Can you stay out of technology for 30 minutes in the morning? It may not be as simple as it seems, since you, like many others, maybe using your mobile phone as your alarm clock. The trouble is that once you turn off the alarm, you've got your phone in your hands, and that means, within 30 seconds of waking up, you've got your first decision: do I check my email or social media? And that, in turn, means you've already been well immersed in your willpower. You're already eroding juice out of your day before your feet hit the floor.

I'd suggest buying an alarm clock, then charge your phone outside the bedroom. This one step will allow you to reap huge rewards in how you set up at the beginning of your day. Now, go a step even further avoid mobile, social media, and tv 30 minutes after waking. Your body is going to thank you, your brain is going to thank you, and your family will thank you.

Drop to the stillness.

No preparation, no data mining, just sit back and be still. If there's something you need to do, follow your breath in and out of your body. The brightest minds integrate the practice of mindfulness into their day. Five minutes to allow your mind to focus and to calibrate. This basic practice will have a significant and meaningful effect on the rest of the day.

Appreciate your adventure. After five minutes of silence, think of three things you're looking forward to today. Write it down and enjoy it. Look for new things you're looking forward to every morning. It could be as simple as your morning cup of coffee or as thrilling as a new first date. This reflection sets the brain to the point of success. It helps your brain look for good things, and in exchange, it will keep on looking for more good things during the day.

Engaging in something that makes you happy when you first wake up will set a positive tone for the rest of your day. If you have it in your mind that your morning went well, and you were in control of it, then you are more likely to feel in control of any obstacles that the day may present. On the other hand, if you wake up on the wrong side of the bed and start off negatively, that failure will spill into anything else that is challenging throughout the day. This will lead to thinking that you had a bad day.

Two co-workers who have to wake up at the same time to go to the same job with the same tasks to do may have two very different experiences. The first guy started his day off with eggs for breakfast, push-ups, a quick vision board meditation, and some goal setting. The second co-worker woke up ten minutes before he had to leave and ran out the door in a panic.

The first guy sees a car in the ditch and stops to help and call the police. After they arrive, he leaves and heads into work. The second guy gets stuck in the traffic jam that was caused by that accident. When you ask both of the co-workers about how their day went, although they had almost the exact same circumstances, the way each of them started out their day makes the difference between being the hero of the day and having a terrible day where everything just kept going wrong.

What if I'm a night owl?

Many psychologists agree that being a so-called "night owl" is passed down genetically. This does not mean that the night owl can't be as productive as someone who is a "morning person". Instead, you must work with what you were given. If you find it very hard to get out of bed in the morning but feel very productive in the evening, you may be a night person. Don't fight against nature, instead embrace the challenge. This will separate you from all the other night owls who make excuses for their actions, or lack thereof.

If you are a night person, change the way you spend your evening before bed. Instead of trying to get all of your work done at night, spend that time planning your next day. Set your goals, choose your clothes, prepare your lunch, etc. This way, you are feeding your night time mania in a healthy way, and allowing yourself enough energy to be productive during the day.

Nighttime people are known to carry more stress and be more emotionally unstable. However, there is a way to avoid these problems. Give yourself a strict bedtime, allowing your body 6-8 hours of rest before you have to wake up. This will ensure that your brain also has enough time to rest and will help to alleviate any stress. Engaging in the morning meditation and vision board ritual will also put your mind at ease and ensure that you are in the right state of mind to conquer your day. Lastly, be sure to give yourself an hour or more to get ready in the morning before you have to leave or start work.

Create your own "workday."

More likely than not, you are an entrepreneur who runs their own schedule. If this is the case, then you are the envy of most. Everyone wants to be their own boss so that they can work from home, watch movies, and eat bonbons all day. Right? This is so far from the truth!

As someone who works for themselves, you know how daunting it can be to make your own schedule and stick to it. This is why most people work for someone else. However, being in the top 1% means that you have to master your schedule and optimize productivity if you want to scale your business. You can't work the same number of hours as your competitor, or you will never get ahead. The question becomes, how can you work MORE when you have the same number of hours in a day as everyone else?

While everyone else sets aside an 8-hour "marathon" of work to do every day, you can create a series of "sprints" within your day to optimize the work that you can get done. Ed Mylett introduced the idea of running 3 "mini days" in a 24-hour period. Given that there are 18 hours in a day that don't include sleep, you can split that up into three 6-hour days.

Do you know those days where you get more done in a few hours than you usually do in a full 8-hour day? Why not leverage this, and create a series of two or three mini days, in which you can maximize productivity and attain several goals within a full day. Think of track and field, where you can run a series of different shorter events and win multiple medals in one day, versus the marathon runner who will only finish one race and potentially get one medal.

Your first mini day should begin right when you wake up. Set yourself two to three bigger goals for the day, and give yourself an allotted amount of time to complete each one. Divide your time accurately, and be in the ultimate hurry to finish each task. This practice will make you more accurate at setting goals, will allow you to expect more from yourself, and ultimately allow you to achieve more within a single day than 99% of the population.

Chapter 3 - Revise your Mission statement frequently

The Mission Statement focuses on the present; identifies the customer(s), the key processes, and informs you of the required level of performance.

The Vision Statement concentrates on the future and is a great source of inspiration. It often describes not only the future of the organization but also the future of the society in which the organization hopes to bring about positive change.

Every brand should have a good mission statement by which they stand. Great brands write mission statements that capture the essence of the company's philosophies and goals. The mission statement should help the target audience to identify with your brand, making it easier for you to create a marketing campaign around. If you are new in business, you should make sure that you have a strong mission statement that coincides with your brand's niche.

It is important that you, as an individual or as a growing company, create and revise your mission statement because this is what gives your brand a purpose. It tells your team and your target audience what you are all about, which will help them to better identify with you. When you have a team that can relate to you, you will have people who will help more, try harder, and become loyal. When you have an audience that can relate to you, you will have customers that will trust you, buy more, and recommend your products and services to other people.

This is a snowball effect that will help your company grow and scale in a way that no amount of money spent on ads can do. Integrity, consistency, and transparency are all core values that you can reflect your audience through your mission statement.

Is your mission statement still valid?

Your firm has been around for a few years, so is your original mission statement still valid? It's important to examine how the current business model and plan matches up with the mission statement you started with. Things are shifting; businesses are evolving, and (hopefully) goals are being achieved. With all this in perspective, you might be shocked to know that it's time for even a mission statement to be revised.

So, what is the Mission Statement?

Even if you've never written an official mission statement, it's highly probable that your business already has an "unwritten" mission statement. At its core, a mission statement is fundamentally known as a formal summary that outlines the objectives and values of a company, entity, or individual.

Questions that you should ask when creating a mission statement.

- What is the value of the business to both customers and employees? This will help the target audience to identify with your brand.

Essentially, the values of your company are the beliefs, ideologies, and principles that drive your business. They have an influence on the employee experience you deliver and also on the partnership you develop with your customers, partners, and investors.

Your company values are the DNA of your business and help

you distinguish your business from the competition. That's why you can't make any strategic business decisions without thinking about them. Your company values are the core of your business.

Apart from helping your employees to live up to the values of your company, it is essential to make sure that your customers know what your core values are.

Evidently, the principles of the company allow you to explain the identity of the brand and to educate the clients on what the company stands for. A collection of common and special core values can be a highly competitive edge. Think about it: if you manage to build a relationship with your clients depending on the beliefs you share, you're most likely to boost this relationship because it is established on common beliefs and principles.

- Why are you in this business? What was it that ignited the spark? This is important to know so that you can keep the flame burning when things get tough.

It takes a lot of confidence to start a business of your own. There are so many uncertainties out there; no guarantee of success, no matter how perfect your idea may be. Starting a company is like taking a leap of faith; and because of the uncertainty, many aspiring entrepreneurs will never take the risk. So what's the thing that drives the driven? What's going to make the entrepreneur step out on a limb, and take that leap? These are the questions that you need to answer without a second thought. Let me share the story of a very famous tech genius on his

"Why" he starts his company. He said, "To follow the beat of my own drum." He went on to say, "After experiencing a few key moments in the lives of some of my family members, I knew that to be in control of my future, I would need to have my own business. I had an uncle who owned his own business and was able to retire at the age of 45. On top of that, he owned a house on a beautiful lake and spent his winters in tropical locations. On the other hand, my parents were both laid off in their 50's. After a period of 17 and 20 years, my parents were forced to start over. It showed me that to fully have financial freedom and control my future; I had to own my own business. On the positive side, my parents are now investors in my company, and I hope my company will help them retire comfortably." So, why did you start your business?

- What makes your brand different from all the other brands in your niche?

Originality: First of all, the brand needs to be original. If you're trying to mimic a competitor's brand, people won't have a logical reason to choose you instead of another brand. If your

message relies on clichés and sales talk, it won't strike a chord with any of your clients. Instead, find an angle that no one has taken before, and create an image and a voice that is entirely your own. That's easier said than done, of course, but it's a basic requirement if you don't want to blend in with the competitive environment.

Integrity: Next, your brand needs to demonstrate a level of sincerity. If you reply to all your social media clients with the same copied and pasted corporate response, people will see you as a faceless machine that cares only about making a profit. Show your human side instead. You

might make some mistakes along the way, but your customers will be able to build a much stronger relationship with you in the near future.

Understanding: The largest and most successful brands are those who know their target audiences. They show this by creating messages that are relevant to only one target niche; for instance, if you target "parents", you might mention a common parenting issue, such as having trouble with a daily routine. This will show a level of sympathy and make it easier for that audience to connect with you. This will result in increased interactions with your brand over time, which in turn will lead to more traffic and conversions. Ensure you study your demographic target carefully and on a continuous basis, and modify your vocabulary and marketing as required.

Boldness: Risk also sometimes leads to reward in branding. The boldest brands are not afraid to experiment with innovative methods or to take a stance on divisive topics within the industry.

They are very polarizing, which means they may alienate a portion of their audience, but they also inspire more loyalty and appreciation from the people around them, and they never run the risk of being seen as "boring" or "just another brand."

Consistency: If your brand expectations are not clearly established, or if you have several people implementing these standards to varying degrees of effectiveness, you can end up alienating your audience. The aim is to get your followers and readers to hang around for as long as possible; but to do that, you have to give them a sense of comfort and predictability. The best way to achieve these attributes is to secure your brand expectations early on and to ensure that all team members working on your campaigns are qualified to carry them out.

Visibility: Clearly, if people don't see your brand, they won't be able to react to it in any way. Although some potential customers will undoubtedly get involved in organic searches as well as other inbound routes, the only way to grow your reputation from scratch is to make your brand as noticeable as possible. Exploit different opportunities to enhance your approach; for example, you can post content on online platforms to develop your brand, launch a social media campaign, or invest heavily in advertising and promotional materials. The fundamental thing is that you need some platform to help your messaging — otherwise, it doesn't matter how compelling the messaging is.

Value: Brands can also stand out by providing more value than their competitors; this can be done in a variety of ways. First of all, you could simply offer better products and services; if you sell a similarly valuable product at half the price, it is only a matter of time before people start gravitating to you.

Regrettably, most companies do not have the versatility to make this competitive (without eating into profits). Alternatively, you could deliver value in terms of quality, more insightful content, or greater dedication to personalized customer support. Originality plays an important role here as well, so consider deeply about how best to appeal to your customers.

If you're just beginning to build a brand, you should be guided by these factors in its development. If you already have a brand, and it seems to be lacking, consider implementing a rebranding campaign, or at least adjusting the execution of your brand standards to reflect those values. At the very least, take a moment to audit your existing brand plan and review your compliance with the expectations you previously set.

When am I supposed to review my mission statement?

Once you have a strong mission statement, you should take the time every quarter to review and revise it to make sure that it is still consistent with your brand. Note any changes that you made or want to make within that quarter and make sure that your mission statement reflects that.

When a company makes changes to its mission statement, this usually indicates growth.

You should make adjustments to your business as it scales, so if you are planning to grow quickly, then plan on modifying parts of your mission statement frequently. This could be changing things that are not working or elaborating on things that are working well.

Ideally, you're going to revisit your business mission statement regularly as your business is constantly living its brand. If it's been a few years since you last carried out a mission statement audit, then it's reasonable to assume that a few changes or improvements may be needed. Here are some other significant events that could cause the need for a re-evaluation:

- The products and services that you offer are different or have undergone significant changes.
- The company is growing and increasing its reach.
- Your business has been modified by political, social, economic or other developments.
- Leadership has changed in recent years.
- Your business has fulfilled its current mission statement.

However, this list is hardly comprehensive, so be sure to evaluate your own business and its specific characteristics.

Here are some examples of powerful mission statements from large online companies and brands.

Amazon: "To be Earth's most customer-centric company, where customers can find and discover anything they might want to buy online, and endeavors to offer its customers the lowest possible prices."

LinkedIn: "To connect the world's professionals to make them more productive and successful."

Facebook: "To give users the power to share and to make the world more visible and connected."

Twitter: "To give everyone the power to create and share ideas and information instantly, without barriers."

PayPal: "To build the Web's most convenient, secure, cost-effective payment solution."

Forbes: "To deliver information on the people, ideas, and technologies changing the world to our community of affluent business decision-makers."

Microsoft: "To empower people and businesses across the globe to realize their full potential."

Revising your company's mission statement is significant, mundane, satisfying, and frustrating at the same time. It's hard enough to fit everything an organization does in one short sentence, much less with the other people in your organization. Reviewing a mission statement allows an organization to remain innovative and valuable to the society in which it operates.

Chapter 4 - Social Media Marketing

Lots of new businesses are birthed all over the world every month. Aspiring entrepreneurs with minds full of entrepreneurial spirit and brilliant ideas turn their perception of the consumer or business challenge on the market into a new product or service solution. However, there is more to set up a business or launch a new product than a reasonable idea and a market in need of a solution.

What do you need to do before you start a social media marketing campaign?

-Test and scale: try every platform of social media. Post as much as humanly possible on each one to create a presence on each platform. See where people are responding the most, and where you are getting the most sales/business from.

-Once you find the top 3 social sites that are making the most noise, capitalize on those by doubling the amount that you are posting. Use these three platforms for paid advertising now that you know they are working.

- Keep the other social platforms going, perhaps outsource those social sites to other people as they are not as important

-Take advantage of scheduled posts on sites like Facebook. This allows you to write multiple posts at once and schedule them to be posted at a later time. You could spend one day scheduling posts for the following week if you wanted to

-Social media is free. If you make enough noise, people will hear you. Once your name is out there, you just have to offer the people something they are already looking for.

-Do hashtag searches for your niche and use the heck out of them every time.

-Invite as many people as you can to like your pages, it's a numbers game, and it's something you can control if you put enough time into it.

-Take advantage of influencers. Collaborate with those who already have a large following to get more eyes on your business

-Use some paid advertising using targeted marketing on social sites like Facebook and Instagram

- YouTube is the second largest search engine and is also known to be a social media platform. Use this to your advantage by putting together short video tutorials if you can, or informational videos explaining something that people want to know more about.

-Be sure to be on as many platforms as possible to expand your horizons. This also protects you against one or many of the platforms possibly shutting down one day. If you put all of your eggs in one basket, then your business could go under just like that.

-Use different types of media. For every video, you can also have a podcast, a written post, a Tiktok, a YouTube video, etc. This will cover all of your basis and reach the maximum amount of people possible. Your goal is to be heard by as many ears as you can.

Several startups score well with the solution they have designed to bring that product or service to market, including supplier logistics, manufacturing, and distribution. But one of the main challenges in developing a new marketing business center is: "We have a great product, but how do we get people to buy it?"

Over the years, I've had the opportunity to talk to a lot of entrepreneurs with great ideas and brilliant thinkers about engineering, artistry, and accounting. Many do not have the same marketing expertise. Particularly in specific areas such as social media marketing. In a mall recently, I overheard a business development manager meeting with a woman who wanted to start a new business with a distinctive line of upscale tea. With a compelling product and business plan, the only lingering questions seemed to be about things like websites, blogs, and social media. Publicity, Keyword research, and product sampling were mixed with other marketing and advertisement principles as if they were all the same thing. I could understand why she was unsure, considering so many possibilities and factors. When contemplating how to introduce a new product or service to the consumer, there are a variety of serious challenges that social media can help address for a new business owner:

Who is addressing the problems that your product solves?

Where do they discuss it and what language do they use?

Who are the influencers aggressively able to influence the visibility and use of the product?

To help answer these key questions, there are three ways that entrepreneurs can use social media to gain insight, raise awareness, and optimize their online marketing.

Listen for awareness – Social media analysis is an ongoing effort to ascertain trends in online interest and hits on a specific matter at a given time. Our upscale tea entrepreneur might need a basic tool like social mention, a mid-market tool like Trackur, or a sophisticated tool like Radian6 to uncover discussions from real customers as they talk about their favorite teas, where to find them, what they like, and what they wouldn't like. Social listening will help to discover other key insights that could promote social media outreach, content, and interaction to raise awareness of upscale tea.

Social media research and analysis are also useful for recognizing relevant influencers. In every online culture, some people make suggestions that others listen to and act on. In combination with group engagement, social listening tools, and influence monitoring services such as Klout, Kred, Traackr, or Followerwonk.

Marketing Social Content – Marketing Social Content also starts with a blog where entrepreneurs can talk about the story of their business and how it solves major market problems. The blog can also function as a communication channel for other blogs in the industry, the media, customers, and other stakeholders.

Our upscale tea entrepreneur could start a blog featuring new teas and welcome conversations with customers and tea fans in general. The blog could serve as a living FAQ database and as a hub for other social interaction channels, including Twitter, Facebook, and Pinterest. Blogs are also effective marketing tools to encourage new buyers to search for goods and services actively. What better time to make it easier than when consumers are deliberately searching for it? Discoverable and shared content makes the social web go 'round.

Monitor, assess, and fine-tune – Social media data management and optimization is a rising trend for successful businesses and taps into marketing performance data and web analytics to reveal insights into the effectiveness of specific messages, media, and promotions. These data-driven findings can provide direction for maximizing social media marketing efforts to boost performance, whether they include different topics for blog posts, words used in tweets, or types of images shared with Pinterest. Google Analytics is an easy choice for start-ups because of its free cost and robust features, including some social media-tracking integration.

The vast amount of information generated and promoted on the social web can be overwhelming. With the relevant questions and tools, entrepreneurs or business marketers with businesses of any size can leverage that data and people-to-people connections to fully understand the digital marketplace, the voice of customers who can influence sales, and keen insight to enhance marketing performance. If you're an entrepreneur, how did you leverage social media to launch a new product or service? What was by far the best (and worst) advice you've received?

In conclusion, Social media is such a great tool in so many ways. We can reach people worldwide, and we can target the audience that we want to reach through paid advertising on sites like Facebook and Instagram.

The effectiveness of social media marketing lies in the right blend of successful strategies. The wrong combination simply reduces traffic from targeted customers rather than attracts them. If you develop your social media campaigns, such as social media optimization, based on existing trends, you can maximize profits and successfully use social networking sites for marketing purposes.

If you're still observing the old social media marketing strategy, it's time to develop different approaches based on all these current trends. It is easier to entrust this exhausting job to a trustworthy social media marketing firm that offers effective social media marketing services than to seek to implement strategies alone. Social networking is a modern age of communication and transfer of information. You must not stay behind in the competition and use this technology wisely.

Chapter 5 - Work on your business (not in it)

When you first start an online business, it usually begins as some sort of side hustle to bring in extra income. Once you realize the potential of your business, you begin to want to grow it into a full-time source of income. This often leads to wearing many different hats and fulfilling many different roles in your business to save you money. That is a great way to start, but it will eventually catch up to you and impede your potential to scale.

An entrepreneur starting their own online business spends on average 60% of their time working on the business' operations. This is a surprisingly large amount of time that could be spent instead, on being a leader for the company, and working on its growth.

When you reach a point where you are spending most of your time working in your business as an employee, this is a very good indicator that you are growing and that it is time to outsource some of the jobs. The earlier you can start outsourcing jobs within your business the sooner you will be able to scale and focus on the things that are important as an owner, which will bring in more customers and more revenue.

How to start automating your business

The first step to start automating your business is to keep a record of all the tasks that you are already doing in a month. Whether it is bookkeeping, product research, fulfilling orders, answering emails, etc. you should keep track of the things that you spend your time doing. After you have these things recorded, you will know how often you do each task, and how much of your time is taken up doing each one. This will be the main indicator of which tasks will be worth outsourcing.

Make a spreadsheet of your "to-do" list and indicate the name of the job, a brief description of what it involves, how much time it takes to complete, and the date. Every time you have to do a particular task, you should record it on your spreadsheet, and at the end of the month, you will have a total amount of time spent on each task.

Based on practice, you can start outsourcing your tasks based on the most time spent doing a particular job. At the end of the month, you should put the jobs in order from most time spent to the least time spent. You will be able to see which jobs you spend most of your time working on. You will be surprised at which jobs take you the longest to do versus the importance for you to do that job. Note that some of these tasks can include things in your personal life that you don't have enough time to do.

The next step is to take a step back and look at the items that you don't want to outsource. This can be tricky, especially for creative entrepreneurs who typically think that their way of doing things is the best and most efficient way. This can make it difficult to want to allow someone else to do a task for you. However, you must evaluate whether or not each job is necessary for you to do and how subjective the task is.

If you have a task like choosing a product for your next launch, then you should probably leave that for yourself because it is an executive decision that should be made by the leader of the company. On the other hand, outsourcing client emails and reminder calls might be something that you can outline for someone else. Always remember that you can go into as much detail as you want when giving someone else a job to perform.

Create a budget

Once you have taken a look at your list of tasks and evaluated what you should be doing and what you can outsource, it is time to create a budget. Although it would be nice to have your entire business automated for you, it is not always financially feasible or even responsible. When you are creating your list of tasks at the beginning of the month, set yourself a budget based on your business' income.

This money should come out of your salary, and not from the money you typically reinvest into your business every month. This is an additional expense which you will want to have some money set aside for so that your company doesn't have to suffer next month when it goes automated. Once you have things in place and your business is earning more, you can re-evaluate your business' budget and use that money to pay for your virtual assistant. This will become a regular business expense, and you will not need to take money out of your income any longer.

You can put anywhere between 5-25% of your earnings towards automating your business, depending on how much your business is making and how much help you need. Make sure that you weigh this amount of money against the price of a virtual assistant to ensure that this is a good business decision. If it costs far more to hire someone than the amount you can save in a month by setting aside this money, then you may want to wait until your business is in a better position to hire an employee.

The good news is that you will most likely be paying someone on an hourly basis. This means that the amount that you will spend will directly reflect the number of hours you will have someone working for you. If you can't afford for someone to alleviate all of the tasks that you had set out, then you can start with one or two jobs and grow from there.

Create training videos

Now that you have a budget in place and a list of tasks that you would like to outsource, it is time to record each task and create a descriptive outline of what each one involves. For each task that you want to hire, you should write an outline of what needs to be done. Then you can screen record what exactly you are doing. This will help the new staff member to see all the stages involved.

For each video that you create, be sure to give context to what they are doing so that they can use their troubleshooting skills if a problem should arise. You can write this at the beginning of the outline so that it is very clear before they learn how to do the job.

The next part of the training is the standard operating procedures. This is a step by step guide which will show them everything that is involved in each job. This can be either a voice-over in the video, a written version, or both.

Once you have finished, you will have a series of videos along with instructions for one or multiple employees to follow. If you have all of the systems in place properly, then you should have consistent work even if someone leaves and you have to hire a new employee.

A great example of a company that does this well is McDonald's. Their standard operating procedures are so precise that they can hire a 15-year-old off the streets and have them making the same quality foods with extreme consistency within a few days working. Although their turnover rate is high, they have such amazing systems in place that they can simply plug in a new employee with no interruptions in production or service.

Share the vision

Be sure to share your mission statement with any new team member that you hire on.

Even if their task is mundane and seemingly unimportant to the bigger picture, sharing your mission statement will allow you to build some rapport with your employee, and will also actually help in the hiring process because you will be able to find someone who matches your brand's personality by keeping this in mind. Including your employees in the bigger picture will also create a lasting relationship and make them feel like a team member. There will also be a bigger chance that they will become loyal to your brand, and recommend you to their friends and family.

The hiring processes

There are many ways that you can find a virtual assistant to alleviate some of your tasks.

One of the best places online is w ww.upwork.com. This is a website for freelancers where they can advertise their skills and find work. Another great thing about this site is that you can make a job posting. This will allow you to interview several different freelancers on one website and see who will be the best fit.

Create an interview sheet. You should include a bullet point list of things that you expect from an employee. This can be anything from personality traits to previous work experience. Your interview sheet should also include a list of questions that you can ask over the phone or on skype. It is always better to speak to someone over the phone rather than through email or messenger. This will allow you to see if their communication skills are up to par and give you a better gauge of their personality.

Interview Sheet

	Applicant interview sheet Position- Virtual Assistant	
Applicant Name:		
S/n	Questions	Comments
	Operational and Situational questions	
1.	What would you do if you had an urgent question, but couldn't find anyone online?	
2.	What will you do if you were working under a tight deadline and your computer crashed?	
3.	You need important information from a co-worker who's in a different time zone and won't be available for the next four hours. How and when do you choose to communicate your request? Why?	
4.	How would you organize employees' contact information (e.g. in a spreadsheet) to ensure you have all the necessary information in-hand and updated?	
	Role-specific questions	
5.	How do you ensure accuracy in routine tasks such as processing expenses and preparing reports?	
6.	What calendar management tools have you used?	
7.	What's your familiarity with online group communication tools? (e.g. Skype, Hangouts, Slack)	
8.	Describe the steps you'd take to plan a meeting for ten people.	
	Behavioral questions	
9.	How do you stay motivated during repetitive tasks?	
10.	Do you have experience working as part of a distributed team or working remotely? What do you think are its biggest challenges?	

Remember that employees can be a pretty big expense in your

business, so take your time and do your research when it comes to hiring. Coworkers can also make or break a company. If you hire someone who doesn't get things done on time, yes you can always rehire, but this will put you behind on schedule and possibly cost you a lot of money.

Other places to look

There are many other places that you can find quality virtual assistants from around the world. Ensure you evaluate all of your options and choose the best one. Looking at many different platforms will give you a good idea of the quality of work you can get for the best price.

Here is a list of great websites for hiring freelancers:

www.upwork.com - This site has been around for many years and is a reputable place to find

virtual assistants.

w ww.fiverr.com - This site has freelance workers who start at a very low price and offers

workers on a "per job" basis if you need someone to fill in the gaps (when someone quits for example).

w www.getmagic.com - Magic provides text-based virtual assistance for handling all kinds of

business and personal activities — like having a personal assistant for all your needs! Most companies use Magic to outsource their marketing, customer support, and administrative tasks.

w www.virtalent.com - Virtalent is a UK-based virtual assistant company that helps small business

owners hire skilled virtual assistants for clerical jobs.

w www.fancyhands.com – Fancy Hands is a US-based virtual assistant company for businesses

looking to outsource tasks like booking reservations, handling phone calls, and other personal tasks.

w www.virtualstafffinder.com This Philippine-based virtual assistant company is perfect for small

business owners seeking to outsource administrative work. It's best suited for businesses looking to employ virtual assistants on a long-term basis.

w www.247virtualassistants.com - 24/7 Virtual Assistant is a virtual assistant company that offers virtual support for personal tasks such as delivery services and ticket booking. It also offers business management assistance, email marketing, website and search engine optimization services.

Chapter 6 – Invest and reinvest (where to put your money within your business)

Once your small business starts to generate profit, what will you do? The more irrational among us may decide to spoil themselves with dead-end purchases or luxury goods. Although these extravagances are tempting, they are inimical to long-term development.

Reinvesting small business profits back in the business is the best way to ensure its survival. Although more short-sighted business owners may grow apathetic once they begin to make substantial profits, every successful entrepreneur should think of the future when considering where to allocate their new cash inflows. If your business has recently become commercially viable, you may consider reinvesting your profits to accelerate development. To further ensure that you spend wisely, in this chapter, I want to discuss how to put your money to work.

You need to prepare first.

The superstar entrepreneur that you follow on Instagram just posted about the new video cameras that she bought for her business. Your favorite Facebook forum is buzzing about running Facebook ads. And your BFF's business has just expanded its product line to include a large inventory order.

So, does that mean it's time for you to pick up new video cameras, copy brainstorm ads, or order more inventory? Sorry to be a buzzkill, but no. Not without a plan, at least.

If investing in your business is something you're dying to do, or something you're pursuing with a heaping dose of apprehension, doing background checks ahead of time can help ensure you're making the right choice for your business. There are three major issues to consider when deciding whether you're prepared to invest money back in growing and scaling up your business.

Here's what you'd like to know before you invest in your business:

- The finances of your business
- Your finances;
- Your goals

Once you have a good understanding of all these three key factors, you'll be in a better place to make the appropriate calls about how much to invest back in your business.

Is it time to invest?

With several things to consider, there is no straightforward answer as to whether it is the best time to invest in your business or what the best investment is for your particular business. It will always depend on your business' finances, your finances, and your goals. If you're pleased with where your business is, and you're not especially interested in scaling right now, that's great. Not every business needs to expand and scale, and you shouldn't let FOMO-inspired internet users persuade you otherwise. If, on the other hand, you want to develop your online business, and you have the capital to invest? In addition to what to understand before investing in your business, I'd love to provide you with the information required to make sound decisions that will benefit your business and review it as needed.

The Warren Buffet ideology

For decades, business tycoon Warren Buffet, chairman of Berkshire Hathaway, has strongly advised reinvesting small business profits to help launch fledgling businesses. For Buffet, the logic is simple: compound interest leads to rapid growth. When small enterprises take their early net profits in year one and reinvest them in capital improvements, a higher rate of return is generated over time. By year ten, the worth of those reinvested profits will far exceed what it would have amounted to in year one.

Reinvestment

We are often asked: what is reinvestment? In several cases, aspiring business owners and new entrepreneurs have not taken the time to learn about the intrinsic worth of reinvesting profits. In simple terms, reinvestment occurs when net profits (i.e. revenues left over after all operating costs and overheads have been paid) are retained and invested in activities or expenses that are intended to increase the value of the business. Alternatively, reinvestment may also involve cash payments to shareholders in the form of a dividend. Small business owners typically struggle with the former — using net income to increase the value of the business over time. Reinvested income is not taxed as a business expense.

How to Reinvest Your Profit

The decision is not always so clear-cut as to where you can put your money to work. Depending on the growth stage of your business, you may be best served by starting small and upgrading servers and hosting on your website. Or, conversely, it may be smarter to hire a high-level employee or even to purchase one of your competitor's assets.

Below, we're going to break down the top five places where gains will be spent when reinvested. While it may involve making a small pay cut, cycling cash through the business can go a long way towards ensuring future growth.

Marketing and advertising

There are hardly any items in the budget of a small business that is more pertinent than marketing and advertising. Today, digital marketing is rapidly becoming a requisite for small businesses to enter the market and capture a considerable portion of their market share.

A marketing strategy is a must-have for business owners. The only drawback, however, is that using traditional marketing platforms can be expensive. So that's why online digital marketing has become one of the most cost-effective means of increasing the exposure of a small business. Today, the marketing strategy for small businesses should include the following elements:

- Search engine optimization (SEO)
- Content marketing (blogs, videos, etc.)
- Affiliate marketing
- Influencer marketing
- Facebook and Google ads
- Email marketing

As digital technologies become more widespread, digital marketing is becoming more and more potent. For example, 87 percent of U.S. Internet users or more use Facebook. Who wouldn't want to exploit the demographics of that market?

Investing in outsourcing

Outsourcing is another viable strategy for reinvesting business profits. As you might already know, the business dynamics of these days are susceptible to rapid and unexpected shifts. This means that many businesses need to re-adjust their strategies and solutions to suit changing customer preferences and buying decisions that are driven by market trends.

This also calls for drastic organizational changes, which many business owners can not manage. However, because of improved computing power and faster Internet connections than ever before, a real fix has emerged to help businesses with such occurrences. Outsourcing is a cheaper and more efficient option when it comes to drastic changes. You can outsource almost any business activity, such as marketing, IT services, growth, etc., based on your current needs. It is also a more streamlined way to outsource jobs that you need now than to recruit full-time staff that you do not need in the immediate future.

Profitability is something that every owner wishes and aims for. That being said, profitability can guarantee short-term success if you decide to stop making a concerted effort. That's why it's essential to decide what to do with company profits as well as how to reinvest to ensure long-term success and revenue growth.

Invest in Yourself

Realizing how to reinvest profits in your business begins with knowing your value as Chief Executive Officer of the business. Even if you see your role as more "hands-off" than some other business owners, you will need to prioritize the improvement of your skills and personal assets if you expect the businesses to develop as well.

Chapter 7 - Fall in love with failure

Walter Dandy was a professor at Johns Hopkins University many years ago and was the first to perform surgery on the part of the brain that no one thought could be done. Unfortunately, he watched his first 13 patients die from this surgery. Can you imagine how much this failure could have impacted him? However, Walter understood that you have to take big risks to have big successes. He learned from his failures and is now one of the founding fathers in neurosurgery. We are now able to perform this surgery safely and save many lives because he decided to continue to learn after every failure and pursue this impossible feat. Your mistakes, not your perfect record, make you more desirable as an entrepreneur Failure is one of the most significant and valuable resources of the entrepreneur, and investors know that. We tend to partner with entrepreneurs who have a string of major setbacks behind them, rather than with entrepreneurs who are creating their first start-up, always believing that they are bulletproof. The biggest mistake entrepreneurs who failed "enough" is to rest on their laurels. Entrepreneurs who didn't witness a project backfire when the success was right around the corner won't be trained for the fight. An entrepreneur who has tasted failure, on the other hand, will not stop looking for mistakes. He or she will continue to look for ways to improve, even with funds raised, customers lined up, and income flowing in. Investors believe that their money is perfectly safe in the hands of an entrepreneur who knows how to wait with Champagne until after the sale.

Analyze and Change

Failures are quite often expensive, sometimes frustrating memories. Smart entrepreneurs are tries to apply these concepts to their next project. Our ability to change and develop is at its peak after a horrific experience. If our mistakes don't cause serious damage to us (financial, prestigious, mental, etc.), the chances are that we'll find them in time and fix them.

There are two important things to note about failing in your business. First of all, you are going to fail, and you will probably fail many times. Secondly, the only difference between successful people and those who never make it are the choices they make after they do fail. What are you going to do about it? When you lose at something, you must first analyze what went wrong. You can then change your strategy and try again.

It is so important to do this, instead of hiding from the truth or ignoring the fact that you made a mistake just to save face. The more you talk about your failure, especially to other people in business, the more you can dive in and figure out what went wrong. Be open to getting feedback from others. Ask the person who beat you what they did.

Leverage flaws and accept responsibility

If you are a seller on Amazon or eBay, for instance, you should be looking at all of the negative reviews for the product that you want to sell before you invest. This will help you to determine what the weak points are for this product and where the opportunity is for improvement.

If you have been selling a product for a length of time, the same thing applies. Don't go out of your way to hide all of the negative reviews that you got. Don't dump this product and choose a new one just because there are flaws. Instead, accept responsibility for any negative feedback that you received and use this to improve the product on your next shipment. Learn from the negative feedback to improve the product, and leverage these new improvements to market your product and scale your business.

Analysis Paralysis

One of the worst things you can do for your business is to become paralyzed by choices. Decision making can be pretty intimidating, but every entrepreneur must make important decisions daily. More often than not, we have young entrepreneurs around us, taking in more and more information without taking action.

You can get so caught up in the research that you become afraid to take the necessary steps towards success. This usually happens because of the fear of failure. When you are in "learn" mode, you become so comfortable with the consumption of information that diving in and making decisions becomes paralyzing. The more information that you consume, the less likely you will come to decide because you are trying to know everything about something you haven't even started yet. In most cases, you won't have all the answers until you make your own mistakes.

Three simple steps for easier decision making:

The first move is to figure out what you are looking for. If you are deciding between two different products to sell, for example, create a list of "musts" and verify that both products check out. If they do, move on to the next step.

The next step is to analyze the two products and make a list of things that you don't like about each one. You can give each negative point a weight (scale of 1-5 for the level of importance). Then, you can add up all of the points at the end to see which has a higher number. The product that scores a higher total will represent the one with the most negatively weighted points.

Lastly, when you are making an important decision in your business, you must picture what this will look like long term. Does this product coincide with the rest of your brand? Does this product leave you with other avenues of income? How can you use this product to scale your business? If you can picture a positive long-term outcome with this product, then you can feel confident in your decision.

You will not know what the outcome will be until it all plays out in your business. Because you know how to handle failures now, you should no longer be afraid of failing. Don't get paralyzed in the decision-making process for fear that it won't work out. If you follow all of these steps, you should feel comfortable moving forward with the decision and feel confident that you know how to respond to any failures that will come up in the future.

Check yourself

On the other side of things, you have to keep yourself in check when things are going well. If you haven't had a failure in a while, don't let your guard down. Too often, we see entrepreneurs get comfortable with their success. It's like playing a series of games with another competitor; you win four or five times, so you begin to think that it's easy and you loosen up a little too much. This is when the opponent starts to change their strategy and then all of a sudden, they catch you off guard because they want to win more than you don't want to lose.

There is a reason why the brightest entrepreneurs ordinarily take risks: they understand that this is the key to lifelong success. Here's the rationale. There is one human trait that has been proven over time: being uncomfortable is a necessity for growth. Our lives as entrepreneurs are not a battle between us and the world, but a fight between our safety and our pleasure. We've got to straddle the thin line between the two, and that is why Elon Musk is always pursuing a bigger idea, Tony Hsieh bet the farm on reviving Las Vegas, and so forth. We're not going to pursue more because we're nuts. We're pursuing more because stagnation is death.

If you plan to "relax," then you will do just enough to get by. Comfortable can drag into laziness, soaking up your every action as you settle more and more for "good enough."

Instead, the strength lies in being only uncomfortable enough to cross the line between being safe and endangering all that has been achieved. It's taking the "beginner's mind" to whatever you do and understanding, like Bezos, Jobs, and others, that inquisitiveness and risk undoubtedly fuel lifelong success.

Chapter 8 - Expand Your Brand: In What Other Ways

Have you ever heard of people refer to themselves as "Apple People," "Nike People," or "Trader Joe's People?" That's what brand awareness does to a brand: get involved in consumer lifestyles and buying habits so that they don't have to think twice before being a customer — time after time after time. This chapter will help you better understand brand awareness, develop it among your audience, and develop campaigns that will enable your business to grow and change continuously.

What's brand awareness?

Brand awareness is how acquainted your target audience is with your brand and how well they identify it. Brands with strong brand recognition are typically referred to as "trending," "media-friendly," or simply "mainstream." Establishing brand awareness is beneficial when marketing and promoting your business and products, particularly in the initial stages of your business.

Brand awareness does seem like a vague concept, and it's true. For marketers and business owners out there, who like to measure success with neat and tidy numbers, brand awareness is almost certain to ruffle your feathers. And just because it's not a metric that can be fairly determined, it doesn't mean it does not have value. Brand awareness is highly important for business success and general marketing objectives.

Here's the reason.

Brand awareness promotes trust.

In a world where consumers depend on extensive research and the opinions of others before purchasing, brand confidence is everything. When you have a consumer bond to your brand, it is more likely that you will make repeat sales with little or no forethought – and that bridges the gap between loyalty and trust. Brand awareness creates the trust of that brand. Once you put a proverbial face on your brand name, it's easier for users to trust. Brand awareness initiatives will give your brand the personality and the platform to be authentic, receive feedback, and share a story. These are all ways in which we, as humans, create trust in each other.

The relationship between the human and the brand is no different.

Brand awareness creates an association.

I bet you put on a Band-Aid when you had a paper cut. I'm sure you've "Googled" it anytime you have a pressing query. I guessed when you needed to make a couple of copies, you Xeroxed them. And when you packed up for a fun picnic, I'm willing to bet you got a Coke for a snack.

Am I right, huh? Most likely, But, yeah ... Notice how each of the above terms is capitalized. These are brands, not names or verbs. In brand-less terms, Band-Aid should be tagged as a bandage, Google as a search engine, and Xerox as a copier. But it's far more fun to appeal to the brand itself, even though we're not using their actual product. That's exactly what brand awareness does. It combines actions and products with particular brands, instinctually encouraging us to replace common phrases with branded terms. And while at it, simple paper cuts or picnics do promotional activities for us.

Brand awareness builds brand equity.

Brand equity explains the valuation of the brand, which is measured by the experience of the customer and the overall perception of the brand. Good impressions and perceptions are parallel to positive brand equity, and the same is true of negative perceptions.

Here are some valuable things that come from positive brand equity:

- Higher prices, thanks to higher perceived value;
- A higher stock values
- The opportunity to extend the business by product or service line extensions;
- Wider social impact on brand name perception

How can a brand establish (and enhance) brand equity? Developing brand awareness and actively encouraging positive interactions with the brand. Brand awareness is the cornerstone of brand equity. When a customer becomes aware of a brand, they begin to identify it without additional support, end up buying it, begin to endorse it over other similar products and develop loyalty that not only promotes more purchases but also allows family and friends to make recommendations.

This is why brand awareness is so vital. It builds trust with your customers, induces positive associations, and builds value-added brand equity that enables your brand to be a household name.

How to Establish Brand Awareness

Brand awareness for the audience and the general populace doesn't happen immediately. It doesn't come from a simple commercial or marketing campaign, either. Strong brand awareness is the result of multiple consistent efforts that go beyond trying to get paid users. If you expect to raise your brand awareness by posting a few product advertisements on Facebook, you won't get too far. Not only should the buyer concentrate on the product (not the brand), but there will also be a shortage of impact on the ad beyond basic sales.

Here are some ways to create a solid brand awareness base and make a lasting impression on your audience:

Be a person, not an organization.

Once you get to meet a new friend, what do you like to find out about them? I always like to learn about hobbies, aspirations, likes and dislikes, and more. I'm also paying attention to how they talk, what they like to talk about, and what kind of stuff they get excited about.

These are the features that your brand should establish and promote on its own. To leave an impact on your audience, you have to define yourself as more than a company that sells things. How have you've defined yourself? Which words would you use if you were to present your brand to a new friend?

Socialize

Introvert or extrovert, vocal or silent, all humans profit from social interaction and spend time with each other. This is how we stay connected, learn new things, and become known to others. The same should go for your brand. If you're just trying to communicate with someone when you're trying to make a sale or get money, you're not going to be recognized as anything beyond a single-minded businessman.

You need to be social to improve brand visibility—post on social media about things that are related to your product or services. Interact with your prospective customers by responding to questions, commenting on posts, or retweeting or sharing content that you like. Handle your social accounts as though you're a person trying to make friends, not a firm trying to make money. Study shows that over 50% of brand reputation comes from online sociability. Being sociable contributes to greater knowledge and simply to be recognized.

Tell a story.

Storytelling is an extremely effective marketing tool, whether you're selling goods or promoting your brand. Why? Because it's giving your audience something real to latch on. The creation of a narrative around your brand humanizes it and gives it depth. And incorporating that narrative into your ads implicitly promotes your brand alongside your services.

What is your storyline supposed to be about? Everything, as long as it's true. It could be the story of your founder or the story of how your business came up with its first product idea. People like to hear stories about each other. Authenticity is powerful and can lead to a major boost in brand awareness.

Make it easy to share.

Whatever your industry, product offering, or marketing strategy, make it easier for the public to share your content. It may be blog posts, sponsored posts, videos, social media articles, or product pages. It doesn't make a difference what it's like, as long as it's shareable.

Word-of-mouth marketing is the most productive way to create trust and familiarity between customers. If someone notices that a friend or family member is endorsing a product or service, they will take notice of the product and the brand. Is that brand worth exploring? Do they have other great items that I can count on? What are their social accounts like, and what are they talking about? When you make it easy to post about your stuff, potential customers will raise your brand awareness by simply clicking

"Share."

Brand awareness is about impact.

It's about engaging your audience in ways that don't just ask for money, engagement, or loyalty. Imagine that you found someone who wants to be a friend. If they asked for all of the above, you'd probably laugh and pull away, wouldn't you? Not only is this a shallow approach to friendship, but it also leaves no lasting influence on you. The same is true of establishing brand awareness among your potential customers.

How To Boost Brand Awareness?

What about improving your well-established brand awareness and building on that solid base? What will you do as a brand to raise awareness and relentlessly increase awareness?

Here are a few campaign ideas to enhance brand awareness:

Offer freemium.

Freemium is a business brand that provides a basic product or product line free of charge, only for any products not considered to be premium or business-level. It's a standard pricing strategy for software companies such as HubSpot and Trello. Offering a freemium option allows users to get a taste of their brand and product before buying a product. It's a pre-purchase opportunity that can, technically, last forever (as opposed to a free trial that some companies prefer).

It is popular to provide a freemium alternative given that the watermark of the brand is seen on all public-facing sections of the product or service. This is what renders freemium a win-win situation: The buyer will receive the product free of charge, and the company will receive free ads when customers use it. TypeForm is yet another perfect example of this. TypeForm provides a free alternative to its survey program, but customers must have a thank-you page that contains the TypeForm logo and post. This depends on your type of business and product offering; Freemium may be the best way to raise your brand awareness among your audience.

Make free content.

Today, content creation is easier than ever ... and this is a good thing because modern consumers are turning to the Internet for any kind of questions, worries, and DIY projects. Content is a great way to boost your brand's profile, as it's the best way to display personality and discuss ideas and positioning on issues — two main components that characterize and humanize your brand.

Content doesn't have to be printed, either. You can also make videos, infographics, podcasts (which we'll cover below), and more. True, written content like blogs and downloadable manuals are probably the easiest, but they're certainly not the only option. Content doesn't have to stay on your website only. Guest posting and sponsored content will allow you to get in front of different prospects and broaden the type of content you create. If your brand does not create content, you may be missing out on some major brand awareness prospects. Content is a perfect way to authentically communicate with your audience while putting your brand name in front of people.

Sponsor events.

How many festivals, live shows, fairs and exhibitions have you attended? Usually, these sorts of events are not possible without the support of brand sponsorships. (take a closer look at a t-shirt, a koozie, or a string backpack that you probably grabbed from the event. See any brand names?)

Sponsoring events is a sure-fire way to get your brand ahead of hundreds, thousands, or millions of people who are likely to fall into your target market. From posters to leaflets to bottles of water, your brand name will be everywhere if you sponsor an event.

Sponsoring an event also enables you to pin your brand name on an event that suits your personality, aspirations, and inspirations, meaning that consumers will then identify your brand with that event and its aesthetics and character.

Consider Red Bull. Red Bull is an energy drink, so without any attempt to increase brand awareness, we'd only call it an energy drink. But, luckily, Red Bull has brought their promotions to the extreme — literally — by sponsoring extreme sporting activities such as cliff diving and motocross. They're also sponsoring athletes.

Today, naturally, we connect Red Bull with bold and adventurous ... and assume that if we drink it, we will do the same.

Give your brand a personality.

Portraying your brand as a person and describing your narrative are the first steps to give your brand a personality. The next move will be to infuse this personality into the marketing campaigns. To those who market their products and services with personality, you can't help but raise awareness of your brand, because your brand will shine through. Of course, your customers should take note of what you're marketing, but they will also feel your personality through your commercials. It is indeed a smart strategy when you blend. Your traditional marketing strategies include a brand awareness program.

Consider Old Spice. (Did you just visualize a man on a horse? I did.) Their commercials for their hygiene products are full of personality and humor, and they still mention their products throughout. Not only does the commercial have an effect on its viewers, but the mere mention of the "Old Spice Guy" also sends customers back to YouTube to watch the commercial ... and to the store to buy some deodorant.

Produce podcasts.

There is no doubt that podcasts play an important role in our lives ... and marketing efforts. Podcasts used to be a complicated process, produced only by those with a studio as well as a sophisticated microphone. Now, it's easier than ever to make and release a podcast, and doing so will do wonders about your brand awareness efforts.

Why? Because podcasts, like written or visual content, offer an excellent way to connect authentically with your audience. Instead of publicly promoting your product or service (something we have agreed is not the best way to increase brand awareness), podcasts allow you to enlighten, inform, entertain, or instruct your audience and build loyalty by doing so.

Here are a few illustrations of great podcasts created by brands that you know and love:

- #LIPSTORIES by Sephora
- Trailblazers by Dell
- The Growth Show by HubSpot

See how these brands have selected podcast themes that relate to their 1) overall brand message and 2) products or services? Doing this helps them bring the podcast back to their brand and keep raising awareness, too. Creating and growing brand awareness is a never-ending process, just as sustaining a friendship or partnership never ends.

Bolstering your brand awareness through campaigns gives you a chance to tap into marketing and promotional opportunities that you would otherwise not invest in — that is, new, powerful ways to engage the audience.

Measure Brand Awareness

How do you tell if your brand awareness initiatives are going to work? How do you know whether you need to change course, put up with pressure, or address a crisis? You measure it, just like any other marketing metric.

Wait ... I thought you said you couldn't measure brand awareness! Yeah, aha! You've been listening to me. Ok, I appreciate that. You're right — The acceptance of the brand can not be measured traditionally. But you can still look at operations and metrics that will help you measure where your brand stands in terms of popularity and consumer awareness.

Here are some ways to measure your brand awareness and discover where you can adjust your efforts:

Quantitative Brand Awareness Measures

These figures can assist you in painting a picture of your brand awareness. To measure quantitatively, check the following metrics:

It's direct traffic. First of all, direct traffic is the result of people deliberately entering your URL and visiting your website. Your direct traffic number will inform you how much your marketing urges people to visit your website. This is a crucial element, as many customers now find brands via social media, advertising, or typing relevant keywords to your brand or product. When consumers go directly to your site, that means they were already aware of your brand.

Site traffic numbers. This number only represents the actual traffic on the website and can tell you how much of the general Internet population is searching for your content and interacting with your brand. It's not going to tell you where the people came from, but that doesn't matter, because they know enough about your brand to check it out.

Social engagement. Engagement might well relate to followers, likes, retweets, comments, and more. It reflects how many people are aware of and socialize with your brand, as well as how compelling your content is. For example, sites like Sparktoro will give you a specific score for your impact on Twitter.

Qualitative Brand Awareness Measures

This phase is where the "score" of your brand awareness gets a little foggy. But these strategies will also help you determine who and how many people are aware of your brand. To measure qualitatively, try:

Search Google and set up Google Alerts. Doing this will get you up to speed with how your brand is being talked about online. You will be alerted to any news or comments made by a third-party press. As your brand continues to grow, its internet real estate can evolve beyond your website, so keep a keen eye on that.

Social listening. Social listening is the monitoring of social media management tools for organic mentions and interactions. Who tags your brand, mentions it in the comments, or uses your hashtag in their posts? These resources will help you find out. And the more the audience discusses the brand on social media, the more they're aware of it.

Run brand awareness surveys. This process involves receiving direct feedback from your customers and audience, and it can be incredibly helpful not only to understand who knows your brand but also what they think of it. You can release surveys via SurveyMonkey or TypeForm and share them on social media or directly with your users. These quantitative and qualitative practices will help you to understand the awareness of your brand between your audience and the general public. It's never going to be the perfect number, but keeping your pulse on this measure will help you influence campaigns and stay connected to your audience.

In Conclusion, Brand awareness is an important (though

somewhat vague) concept that can have a massive effect on your marketing, customer perception, and sales. Implement these techniques to create and raise awareness for your brand. You will find yourself with a loyal audience that accepts your brand among competitors, prefers your products time and time again, and recommends that your friends and family do the same.

www.ingramcontent.com/pod-product-compliance
Lightning Source LLC
Chambersburg PA
CBHW070252220526
45465CB00004B/1591